BANDAGES OF BONDAGE LORD UNRAVEL ME

BANDAGES OF BONDAGE
LORD UNRAVEL ME

Helen E. Reynolds

Copyright © 2023 by Helen E. Reynolds.

Library of Congress Control Number:	2023909439
ISBN: Hardcover	978-1-6698-7802-5
Softcover	978-1-6698-7801-8
eBook	978-1-6698-7800-1

All rights reserved. No part of this book may be reproduced or transmitted in any form or by any means, electronic or mechanical, including photocopying, recording, or by any information storage and retrieval system, without permission in writing from the copyright owner.

Any people depicted in stock imagery provided by Getty Images are models, and such images are being used for illustrative purposes only. Certain stock imagery © Getty Images.

Print information available on the last page.

Rev. date: 05/30/2023

To order additional copies of this book, contact:
Xlibris
844-714-8691
www.Xlibris.com
Orders@Xlibris.com

CONTENTS

Bandages of Bondage 1
Bandages of Bondage is designed with you in mind. 3
Transparency 5
Dealing and Coping. 7
Let it Go! 9
The Plea 11
I got a bug in me 13
Imposter 15
You Don't Know 17
Real Recognize fake 19
Memories 21
Traveling through time 23
In the closet 27
Poetic Poems of Praise by H.E.R. 29
Blemish 31
The case u must know it's not too late. 33
Attempting to take a step 35
Self-Reflection 37
Life Saver Y'all. 39
The Crave. 41
The Question 45
Arrest my Flesh! 47
With your looking self. 49
Lord I'm Waiting 51
Angela, Angela, My Badu! 53
I See 55
What the enemy meant for my bad! 57
Growing Pains 59
Truth wears no mask! 61
Torn 65
Sabotage 67
Religion Versus Relationship 69

The Analogy	71
Tool Kit	73
Wounded Soldier!	75
The Plea! The Release!	77
The Love Letter!	79
I see the enemy!	81
What do men and women say that I Am!	83
Bed of Affliction	85
I am Me!	87
My Silhouette!	89
Breakthrough!	91
I Am that I Am!	93
Live!	95
Inner Healing!	97
Generational Curse!	99
Dating is so overrated	103
I Still Got A Praise!	105
Soul Ties	107
The Plot, The Plea	109
An open leter to my perpetrator.	111
Wounded By Words!	113
The causation of the Truth!	115
I've Been Searching…	117
I'm bleeding out!	121
I'm married to my husband, I'm miserable and it hurts!	123
I asked my husband to forgive me but I didn't tell him why…	125
I drink and I smoke to calm my nerves…	127
I'm saved but I want to have sex…	129
Stess and Pressure	131
Strong Holds!	133
Paper	135
A Good Guy	137
Victory!!!	139

BANDAGES OF BONDAGE

The chain represents the entrapment of your mind.
Intensive care
Life Support
Flat line
Are all categories that reflect these poems that tell stories
of the process used to resuscitate you.
Throughout this book just like in life you will witness or encounter
and attest that at some point in time you felt like you couldn't
breathe; something, someone is smothering me.
You were just experiencing a relapse.
Another device used to take your life.

Lord unravel me I need a release!

I need a release as I reflect on this piece

I,_____

BANDAGES OF BONDAGE IS DESIGNED WITH YOU IN MIND.

It has no respect of persons
Your original origin is the common denominator.
The Lord our creator
This book was printed to take you back to the beginning
So that you will understand you have purpose and that you are a part of a plan
That's greater than man
Once you open your heart and allow your ear to hear the
deep message that is enclosed in this book.
Grab hold and take this spiritual journey
Deliverance, yokes being destroyed and joy will replace that space.
Faith will be increased
Everything the enemy thought he stole will be replemished
Not a blemish will remain
I declare and decree in Jesus name!
As you take this journey I welcome you to the road to recovery!
Be Blessed!

What my mind is telling me as I reflect and release.

TRANSPARENCY

In my nakedness
It reveals my flaws, my imperfections of this flesh
But it allows me to no longer be comfortable covering up mess
It makes me come clean and face the reality of servantry.
I must be led by the spirit of God in everything that I do
No longer can I operate and function
On the premise of what I want to do
Lord I surrender
Everything, all things unto you.
Years ago when the Lord gave to me
Bandages of Bondage, Lord unravel me
I only had seen his vision through one lens one scope.
But now on today
I can see the range of this gift this thing
It goes deeper than the eye can see
It reveals God transforming me into a state of transparency.
Humbly I say
Lord have thy own way

This piece speaks to me,

DEALING AND COPING.

Boy, I'll tell you this is no joke
It can cause your brain to operate in overload
So much smoke that you can't see reality.
You can't see the person or thing you are becoming
Another setup
To position you for failure and defeat
A plan designed by yours truly the thief
I'm not going to even give that joker a name
Cause it's just insane
How dealing and coping caused me to fall into trying to carry this burden and pain
Dealing and coping is not what my Lord has in store for me
When he can remove it completely
All I and you must do is let it go
Yup that easy
I've released my grip on this stuff
No longer am I dealing and coping
But I'm releasing and increasing my total dependency in you God

Release!

LET IT GO!

Can you see it clearly?
My hands are open
My mind has staged a release of all the clutter and mess that's been smothering me
I'm not holding on to this baggage anymore
The claim ticket don't say the property of my name
As a matter of fact it's marked unclaimed
Why this baggage is going in the trash
Wherever God decides to throw it
I won't be mad
Cause I have truly let it go.

Trash release!

THE PLEA

I believe, I believe
That is my testimony
Then when I'm alone in my mind
I'm trying to figure things out on my own
Lord where did I go wrong
Fix me!
Can't you see that I'm not operating properly?
I continue to lean on my own understanding
Day after day
I continue to pray
Asking you to send help my way
I repent
I confess
I come before you in my nakedness
I lay at your feet
I hear you speak
I attempt to make adjustments and make corrections to fix my imperfections
Lord it's me!
I'm struggling I'm striving to be who and what you intended for me
Sometimes why?
Cross my mind
Why you choose me?
Why you love me?
I don't understand in its entirety your plan for me.
Lord I'm asking and believing you to help me to comprehend the confusion
I Believe

The Mustard Seed is small and underestimated yet it is powerful indeed!

_____
_____
_____
_____
_____
_____
_____
_____
_____
_____
_____
_____
_____
_____
_____

I GOT A BUG IN ME

Lord I got a parasite
And it is killing me and I can not fight
It's eating me up on the inside
It's attacked my heart
I'm falling apart
It's crawling under my skin
It keep peeking his head up causing me to sin
In hopes I won't continue this race and that I'll give up
But oh no you Parasite
I'm going to roll up my sleeves and stay on my knees
I can't give up without a fight
Because I know I have a right to the tree of life
I truly believe that prayer is the key to the kingdom and
This mustard seed faith is guaranteed to unlock the gate.

Now Faith!

IMPOSTER

The perpetrator, the instigator and the mouthpiece.
Yea these are all devices sent by the thief
Some call him the enemy.
I call him the cowardly lion
With a pussycat roar
Always attempting to show you an illusion so that you
won't pursue your God given destiny.
His expectation is for you to jump to conclusions and believe his lies as the truth.
When case in fact he doesn't have the authority to do what he is saying he can do.
Sounds familiar same lie he told since the beginning of time.
Back in the garden of eden he used a serpent to relay his false truths
to lure Adam via eve to abort God's truth and God's rules.
I told the perpetrator. Now let's discuss the instigator.

Be Aware!

YOU DON'T KNOW

You. You. You.
Don't' know
You can't see
What transpired and happened to me
You. You. You.
Can't see the scars that lies beneath
That bare witness
As a constant reminder of dark times
You might have crossed paths with me along this journey
You might have caught a glimpse
Maybe you were present during that episode of so many stories untold
Yet
You. You. You
Don't Know
But after this you will know all that you need to know
So when you look at me don't try to figure it out.
Cause you will be lost no doubt
Just know that there is a God of mercy and grace
Who is Omnipresent?
In whatever state or place you may be in on today
You deliverance is on the way.

No shame!

REAL RECOGNIZE FAKE

I'm not making excuses
I'm just trying to tell you that I've been around for a while
I've done some things
And No I'm not glorifying those things
But I'm merely trying to get you to see
That God is real and he resides in me
Because it took God to deal with me
I was considered what the world calls rough, tough, hard core and all that stuff
But the God I serve was able to break through all the barriers and walls I put up
So no one really knew what was up.
No one really knew I was damaged, hurt, full of pain and shame
Living in turmoil
Caught in the game!
Just as I was
So are some of you today
Sitting here reading while screaming
Wow I can relate!
Because you have been in this state where
The outward appearance is clean cut your sitting
there like you got your stuff in order
When you are really malfunctioning
Stop the charades get out of life's parade
Allow God to set you free
He is waiting patiently.
I know He can. Because He did it for me!
There is nothing like liberty!

Let God set you free. Liberty awaits you. Walk in destiny!

MEMORIES

Deja Vu is nothing more than my mind reflecting back on the things I went through
The mere mention of certain things triggers thoughts, emotions and even old flings
Sometimes it's the smell of an aroma, a song that is being played
That takes my mind back in the day
Reminding me that I too was living in sin and not saved
Oh how I craved whatever my flesh wanted back in those days

Acknowledgement is key!

TRAVELING THROUGH TIME

When the wind blows nobody knows which way the debris will go.
The particles that float sometimes cause those that have allergies to choke
But only for a moment
Then they get a breath of relief and continue on their journey
You and I
He and she
Them and They
Are where we are supposed to be
On this quest to do our best
We are merely traveling through time
No such thing as rewind
Yet you can move swift through time
Although you may miss an intricate moment
If only the time could cease
Be still and yield
So that one could embrace that very special moment
Hold hostage and capture that place that is there today and gone tomorrow
Now only memories reside as you continue traveling through time
Memories represent time passed where the mind has hit rewind
Then pressed play to enjoy but yet a moment captured in that space
To help you realize
Time never waits
So let us make the time you spend here
Worth the memories you will share

The very essence of time.

Can you see?
What really lies beneath?
The fancy clothes, the smile on my face.
I'm in an uncomfortable state.
So much on my plate.
Bills late, children out of control, house on the verge of being sold.
I'm going through just like you, you, and you.
I don't have a clue on how I'm going to get through this episode
I need some relief
The pressure is so overwhelming sometimes I feel like I can't breathe
Like I don't want to live if I got to continue to feel
Depression, neglect, pain and shame.
This is my cry for help!
I'm weak.
Lord if you hear me I need you to help me!

What lies behind your eyes?

IN THE CLOSET

No I'm not a homosexual undercover brother.
But I do have some things in my closet
Overcrowding my shelves.
Anger, low self esteem
I'm suffering because of some things
That happened to me in my youth
Things I thought I buried but somehow they've resurfaced
Now I'm having a difficult time dealing with the truth
I'm hurting, damaged, used and abused and I don't know what to do.
I'm in the closet
Anxiety, frustration, lack of understanding
The pressure to be strong when I'm feeling weak
I need something, somebody, something to grant me some relief
Cause the thief done robbed me.
I'm in the closet
Drugs, Alcohol, Sex
And still I'm drowning in my mess.
So much for the self medication method
I'm hurting and I don't know what to do.
I've tried everything I was big, bad and bold enough to do.
I'm in the closet.
Afraid to come out
I'm feeling like if I could just lift my voice and shout!
Help me!
Please!
Is this a nightmare or just a dream?
This can't be a reality for me!
I'm in the closet.

Silent Screams! What does it look like and what does it mean?

_____
_____
_____
_____
_____
_____
_____
_____
_____
_____
_____
_____
_____
_____
_____

POETIC POEMS OF PRAISE BY H.E.R.

Exhort to acknowledge the truth about what lies in you. Recognizing your self-worth and realizing your true identity. One that gives you inner peace and allows you to live in harmony with the Lord the Creator, your Maker, your Savior.

I was once asked what jewel or gem describes what lies within me? And quickly this poem this piece came flowing through me... entitled **Servant.**

Women we are precious Jewels yet the question remains which one are you?
The thought that came to me was that I am the apple of my heavenly father's eyes.
I'm called, chosen and set aside.
And where I rest rule and abide is on the inside of God's treasure chest.
See he always preserves and keeps the best set aside and secluded.
I'm well preserved and kept for his usage.
I know you are wondering what's my name? Which jewel am I?
It's quite simple.
I am and I go by and can be described as servant.
See I am very rare yet often used as an instrument as his tool.
Jewel is defined by the dictionary as one that is treasured and esteemed.
Yeah that describes me.
I'm treasured and esteemed by my heavenly father the king.
Why? Because when he sees me he sees his righteousness.
He sees his radiant light shining oh so bright.
It's shinier than a diamond that really can't define me.
Yet I possess its clarity and characteristics of stability and its brilliancy.
I'm just his servant.
Pre Destined and designed since the beginning of time.
I'm like the pearl. God's truth formed through suffering, to endure a costly experience. But when God gets through, I'll look up to heaven and tell my daddy that all the honor and glory belongs to you.
I'm just his servant
A woman of virtue. For he already told you that my price is far above rubies.
God's treasure chest.

What lies in me beholds his beauty and his Excellency.
I'm just his servant.
What jewel am I?
Why I am the apple of his eye.
No one precious jewel can describe a servant that's me.
I'm whatever God wants me to be.
A servant indeed.

When God sees me he sees… Yeah and thats what I believe!

BLEMISH

Self Esteem, Oh Self Esteem
Someone wake me from this dream or should I say nightmare.
No one cares. Oh how can I bare to look at this image I see
looking back at me as I stare into the mirror?
Who is this person that's trying to convince me?
That someone actually loves me unconditionally just as I am.
Oh but how I long to see exactly what he sees in me.
Cause right here, right now all I see is ugly me.

Distorted image.

THE CASE U MUST KNOW IT'S NOT TOO LATE....

God specializes in your kind.
Those that is afflicted and stricken with illness and sickness.
Those that are of a low spirit
Whoever you are?
Whatever your story is?
Whatever you have done
Whatever you are planning to do
Just know that God still loves you.
This is your opportunity
To get your breakthrough.
This is the open door to explore what God has in store for you
You've tried just about everything you were big and bad enough to do
So why not choose

The door he left open for you.
Your escape is totally up to you
Choose!

The invitation.

ATTEMPTING TO TAKE A STEP

Something just crept right on in.
Something got me imbedded in my sin
It feels as though I'm in a choke hold
Lord I'm tired of fighting, I'm tired of crying.
I thought I let this thing go.
But it just keeps on coming back and attaching itself to me.
And I keep inviting it to be a part of me.
Lord help me to let it go.
These addictions keep putting me in uncomfortable positions.
Lord if only my eyes could see
The beauty you see in me
Then maybe I'd walk more freely in my destiny
Maybe I'd not hold back due to the lack of seeing what you see in me.
I'd then have the capability to believe then achieve then chase my dreams of being who you want me to be.
Lord help me to trust thee.
I'm attempting to take a step.

God's omnipotence!

SELF-REFLECTION

I picked up the mirror one day because I wanted to see who or what was hindering me. I had to look deep down on the inside to see what was trying to hide from me.

It seemed to be playing peek a boo but I thought to myself I see you. Then it would hit me and say tag you're it. And the struggle continued to afflict my soul, and cause my spirit man to be incapable of expanding and walking in God's divine planning for my life. All because some stuff was occupying that space. Up and down Dr. Jekyll and Mr. Hyde this thing got me on a vertical joyride.

I'm just doing a self-reflection.

As I continued to reflect on me, myself and I looking in that mirror I found anger, unforgiveness and low self-esteem. I was so concerned and consumed about what you, you and you and even you thought of me. That I couldn't see and follow God's direction and his authority over me.

I continue to focus on the reflection of myself in my eyes the images that I see.

Oh no I see Mrs. Vulnerability.

And she is carrying fear and rejection accompanied by the need to be accepted by her peers.

When God makes it clear that he does not give us the spirit of fear but power love and a sound mind. Yet there something going on inside of me that causes me to see the ugliness.

It's just low self-esteem.

Clarity provides peace.

LIFE SAVER Y'ALL...

You see he hung, bled and died for you and I. You can just as I did accept and receive the gift of salvation.
Today I feel like a child walking across the stage at graduation.
He gave his life so that my life your life could be saved and I am indebted to Jesus as his slave.
It's a privilege and a honor to serve so that this life he saved can compel men, women, boys and girls that it pays to live for Christ. My story, my life is a saver.
Won't you make Jesus Christ your choice?

THE CRAVE.....

I'm Saved!
I'm Saved!
Yet, every now and then, I crave those familiar things.
The desire has my flesh on fire. Burning, yearning twitching and turning.
1st Corinthians 7:9
KJV
But if they cannot contain themselves let them marry
for it is better to marry than to burn.
NIV
But if they cannot control themselves they should marry for
it is better to marry than to burn with passion.
NLT
But if they cannot control themselves they should go ahead
and marry. It's better to marry than to burn with lust.
OK.
I just picked up the root of the issue. It's not the fact
that I, you, he, she lack a wife or a husband
It's the mere fact that you and I have been busted.
So don't get disgusted in your feelings, get out of your chest.
Cause I, you them and they are just a ratchet mess.
Full of lust, this is why we struggle with waiting on God
and standing firm with what he has promised.
Lord I need you to empty me out and fill me up. Cause i'm in trouble.
Psalms 141:14 is just for me.
I think I'll feast on this piece from the **ESV**.
Do not let my heart incline to any evil to busy myself with wicked deeds in company with men who work iniquity and do not let me eat their delicacies.
Lord I thank thee for giving me a word just for me. To kill this flesh daily.

Colossians 3:5 ESV
Put to death therefore what is earthly in you sexual immorality impurity passion evil desires and covetousness which is idolatry?
Shout Lord Kill It!
God replies…..
Matthew 17:21
NASB
But this kind does not go out except by prayer and fasting.
Um Huh!
Something so simple yet so profound
Disobedience is lurking around, in you, you and I.
Because we have been told.
Little prayer little power.
We've been told

The Crave continued.

You got to pray if you want to stay
We've been told.
You must fast if you want to last.
He gave B.I.B.L.E
Basic Instructions before Leaving Earth
And we still can't seem to do the God Thing the right way.
Why?
Proverbs 14:12 NIV
There is a way that appears to be right but in the end it leads to death.
Now look at your neighbor and ask.
Do you want to be kept?
It's an invitation.
Do you want to be kept?
Stand to your feet.

Jude 24:25 KJV
Now unto him that is able to keep you from falling and to present you faultless before the presence of his glory with exceeding joy. To the only wise God our Savior the glory and majesty, dominion and power both now and ever Amen.
I leave this final note with you
Romans 12:1 NIV
Therefore I urge you brothers and sisters in view of God's mercy to offer your bodies as a living sacrifice holy and pleasing to God this is your true and proper worship.
We've been told.
We've been warned.
Now it's our turn to apply the teaching. All we have to do is seek him.
Now that you know better.
Do better.
In despite of the crave don't allow your flesh to carry you to hells grave.
I'm just saying what I said…

THE QUESTION

Lord.
Why? Why?
Why do I continue to entertain when the Holy Spirit has made it plain? This guy is not the truth yet he is a lie a substitute. It through him was designed to block you lock you into a trance. It was sent to have you feeling and thinking he could possibly be you man. When in fact he is not a part of God's divine plan for your life. He is darkness trying to shine from the glare of your radiant light. He is drawn to you cause what he sees you possess. Even though he knows he is just a mess.
He pretends to be on the path that God has set when
in reality he is walking in destruction.
Looking, seeking whom he may devour. Because he is not a man of God. He is just a coward putting on a façade. Why he is a phony, a fake, a fraud.
Ladies this piece is not just for you. It also for the fellas
and it goes a little something like this.

This chic is not the wife!
Breast hips legs and thighs butt cheeks yea imma freak. Make you want to know what lies beyond these thighs. Im cute in the face thick in all the places. Umm no you just a hoe a garden tool in the field translation the streets setting up priivate meetings cheating spreading your self so thin then showing up in places wearing various faces trying to deceive me. Listen woman stop rehearsing a scene that you dont qualify to even be in. What you mean. Im glad you asked. My role as the man is to find a wife. Not play in the field.

ARREST MY FLESH!

My eyes are opened. Lord that which was once suppressed is alive and beating.
Trying to hook up secret meetings. Set up, sabotage, and lure me out
of your will. So that it can steal my purpose, ram shack your divine
plans cause me to miss the blessings that you have awaiting me.
If only I will stand still. Obey and stay connected to the source. Jesus Christ it's you.
Lord I'm truly chasing you.
Struggling yet I stand on your promises.

WITH YOUR LOOKING SELF.

Boaz, Boaz.
Where are you? I'm looking to be found by you.
I know I shouldn't be looking but I'm getting impatient while I'm waiting.
What's the hesitation?
I prayed the prayer Lord is he near?
I asked you to prepare me. I gave you my list.
Lord please do it quick.
Well not quick but soon. Well when it's time according to you.
I don't want to get ahead of you Lord and I know you got all things under control.
Well it's just it's just…
Lord I confess.
I've been thinking, daydreaming because I want
someone to share and create memories with.
I want to experience how it feels to be with a man according to your standards.
I see sister and brother doo whoop looking so happy and brother
and sister Winn seem to be working things out again.
So I thought how wonderful is that to stay married to go through and get to
share the ups and downs the late night brawls arguments disputes but at the
end of the night we could just pray our way through. Forgive and compromise.
Lord. I know I know. I'm looking from the outside and what I see are
images in my mind that really only exist in the essences of time.
Desire, Desire. Can send your heart on a rampage cause you to disengage and make
false truths. To the point you won't recognize what's standing right in front of you.
Marriage is work and you not ready yet. So keep your flesh in check.
By the way you failed this test. Cause nothing good dwells in your
flesh. I gotta keep it under the subjection of the word of God.

LORD I'M WAITING

While I'm waiting. I realize the enemy is baiting.
Ordering his imps camouflaged as pimps on the scene demonstrating
the traits of what my eyes and flesh once entertained.
The smell of his cologne was once enough to initiate him and I getting it on.
Oh Lord!
Not another sad love song. An episode that didn't last long.
The enemy is playing on me.
What I really mean is he is pulling my strings.
Because it's obvious I still have some things that are still attached to me laying
waiting for the opportunity to come back and have me act unseemingly.
Yeah it sounds like a trap.
Lord what am I to do when those urges and desires of what I use to
do is still taunting and tantalizing it got my flesh on an uprising.
Wow let me catch my breath. I think I'm breaking out in a sweat.
Silence Saith the Lord!
Resist! Resist!
I said you don't have to accept it.
You know the enemy is coming and he is coming quickly.
So it's not that difficult you just gotta stay equipped armed and alert.
Stop proclaiming yet you still entertaining and that's
why you remaining in the midst of your sin.
I'm talking about the sin that's embedded within.
It's called lust!
My daughter you done got yourself a leech. That's
why you continue and keep stumbling.
The leeches are embedded in your skin attached and is sucking and going deeper
in order to keep you disconnected, off track all designed to set you back.
Now I never promised you that it would be easy.
But I promised you I would never leave you.
And I'm still here.
Every moment, every step of your journey.
All you gotta do is recognize that that I Am lives on the inside of you.
And despite all the temptations, offers that are placed on the table.
You still must choose.

To live and let your flesh die daily.
Stay on the altar fast and pray.
Cause in your case it's the only way.
Same things those ole church mothers would say.
Remains to be true.
If only WE, I, YOU would follow those simple rules.
God made it clear. He left this here B.I.B.L.E
Basic **I**nstructions **B**efore **L**eaving **E**arth
It's your choice!

ANGELA, ANGELA, MY BADU!

This piece was inspired by you.
Happy while she waits, diligently while he seeks.
My sister, my friend.
God the Lord the Creator has the perfect man.
He has the divine plan.
Listening to you pour your heart and soul into getting your story told.
One can call it the silent rebuttal that finally took flight.
You brought your inequalities to the light.
You opened up that cup of corrupt, struggles yet provide the strategies that you have developed and continue to apply as God the Lord the Creator makes you better.
And you become greater in those areas of once called defeat. I like to call it the valley of the thief. That's a place we've all journeyed. Where the enemy the thief has stolen so he thought yours and my destiny. Just know my sister my friend the more we open ourselves up to the Lord to uncover, the more we will recover and he can restore to prepare us for more.
Remember we serve a God of Abundance. So no limits just remember.
To remain happy while you wait and the king he has for thee will be diligent while he seeks to find you and my king finds me.
Single yet never alone because God was there all along.
He heard your cry he sees the rip the tear in your heart.
Your desires requires you to go beyond and deeper beneath what you want to a place of what you need,
God knows and sees yet he still wants the best for you and for me.
I can totally relate to the state of the silent cries created by those on the outside. Their viewpoints, the stares, and the thoughts of what they might have said in regards to your choices and mines to remain single Satisfied and awaiting the divines hand-picked, developed and equipped gentlemen. A perfect fit. Defined by his intent, a husband.
It's on the way.
Don't go astray to what the Lord the creator has to say.
If he said it then it is so.
We have to learn to wait and delight ourselves in the Lord.
As we are under construction.

Wait!

I SEE

I looked beyond what you see and I see the real me.
I see the imperfections, the ugliness.
My eyes are opened wide.
I've opened the hidden secrets buried deep down on the inside.
I see the little girl crying feeling lost unsure of herself empty and full of despair.
She is carrying the weight of the world on her shoulders.
All the debris the residue from all the things she went through.
Mother you asked a question.
What do I see when I look in the mirror?
I see the distorted image.
The brokenness the pain the shame.
I'm not in denial.
I'm not looking to blame or call any names.
What I see is the reality of my brokenness.
I see the shattered pieces
Yet God mercy never ceases.
I see.

When clarity speaks...

WHAT THE ENEMY MEANT FOR MY BAD!

Paparazzi A.K.A. Haters!
I thank you personally for your publicity.
Thank you for pointing out my iniquities. Thank you for the constant
reminder of my struggles, my shortcomings, and my bad attitude.
All the times I just didn't speak to you.
It just kept me on the altar, on my knees before the Lord concerning me.
I congratulate you on today because of your ridicule it
paved the way for me to stay on my face.
Allowing God to break me, make me, mold me bestow more of himself upon me.
With gifts and talents wisdom and knowledge, meekness.
So that I, my life reflects what the scriptures teaches.
I am more than a conqueror through him that loves me.
So keep on professing and confessing that you don't like me but you love me.
That's just a bold faced lie.
Like and Love are intertwined.
They work together like minutes flow through time.
So stop faking, perpetrating and tell the truth.
I just did and this poem is just for you!
Any fans in the house.
Go ahead and shout because the cover has been snatched.
You've been found out.

What the enemy meant for my bad God turned it around and worked it for my good.

Sound Check! Reflect and release!

_____
_____
_____
_____
_____
_____
_____
_____
_____
_____
_____
_____
_____

GROWING PAINS

This piece was inspired by the notion that God creates and we discover.

Growing pains.
Nothing ever remains the same.
All things must change.
Elevation requires a self-evaluation and a determination
to go through the transformation.
Yeah I know it's a lot of tion.
But this process must be completed and get done.
Tion is a suffix that is placed on a word to represent an alteration.
Display a demonstration that reflects a change.
I'm still talking about growing pains.
See no longer am I the same.
As I grow in Christ.
New battles come with each level and each height.
Sometimes I get weary.
Sometimes I feel pain.
Sometimes I feel lost in this spiritual game.
I'm having growing pains.
Lord.
I cry, I pray, I lay out before you begging and pleading for you to deliver me.
From the sin that's embedded in the depths of my soul.
So much in me must come out and I need some relief.
I need true inner peace true joy another dose of
anointing so yokes can be destroyed.
I got some walls that need to come tumbling down.
So I can stand up and say with a smile on my face.
I'm growing through the pain.
While God is plucking off and destroying things in
me that's causing me to feel defeat.
This flesh is fighting against the change.
The enemy is trying to stunt my growth in hopes I'll
throw in the towel and lose all hope.
Oh ye of little faith.

I must continue my journey and complete this race.
This pain I'm experiencing while I'm growing.
Is God showing me that there is so much more he has in store.
He is working on the inner me.
So that what's on the inside can shine through and reflect on the outside.
Growing pains has a purpose you see.
They are helping to develop me into who I'm supposed to be

They are designed to help you reach your destiny.
So now I'm growing through the pain

While going through the pain
I'll never be the same in Jesus name!
Growth has no limits.
Pain is just the result of the process taking place.
I'm going to continue to run this race.
Through my transformation taking place.
Lord I thank you for your Grace.

TRUTH WEARS NO MASK!

Truth wears no mask.
No longer can I hide
No longer can I carry this filthy trash
Molestation a fatherless situation
All these scars that never really healed
Yet they continue to hurt and gather infection.
Antibiotics can't cure the pain.
I refuse to allow this disease to drive me insane
I was molested and it was not ok
But my Lord and Savior hung bleed and died and was pierced in his side
Because he knew I would encounter that situation in my life
He knew that I would struggle and allow this to tug at my mind
He knew the enemy would try to use this to set me
back in time to a place of hopelessness.
He thought it would stunt my growth but the seed that God has planted in me.
Will forever continually grow.
Even while the weeds of my past try to smother what God predestined
What's being developed in my season of harvest.
The garden of my destiny.
God bound forever I will be
Striving to be who He created me to be
Truth wears no Mask!

Sometimes it just make sense to not respond to all the mess.
Especially the stuff folks tend to send to you through a text.
Really!
Take this piece for instance entitled.

Focused!
While traveling...

Your greatness don't justify your lateness
Your rudeness and the mere fact your behavior reflects a person that is clueless
I truly understand and am aware
That there is only one of you and that you are not replaceable
However the object was not to replace you
It was not about you
Confusion.
Don mistake my quietness for acting funny or always doing something.
Extra.
Stop trying to focus on the moves that I make.
Cause make no mistakes
I too possess his greatness
I just understand while pursuing God's divine plan
Folks can't go where God is taking me
It's not personal.
It's how i'm learning to obey him.
So if in fact you feeling like you lack my interaction with you
Just know that I have some things I have to do
That to be quite frank
Don't include you!
P.S.
I still love you boo!

Boundaries!

TORN

I feel torn between my thoughts
I know what I want to do
I´m not lost
Child #1 child #2, child #3 and child #4
Another episode of you reap what you sow
I married a man or should I say a pair of pants
Never acknowledged God
Nor did I wait to see or get a response
I ignored all the obvious signs
But this natural thing called love had me blind
I broke one of God's ultimate commands
Don't worship idol Gods
Yeah that means a man
My ex-husband was my God
It sounds so sick
But I know now that it was all a trick
A trick that was wrapped with a treat
So I thought I had game
But it had me
Don't look at me funny like you never put all yourself into a man
Because you thought you had a plan
Only to find out it was a scam

Confession is good for the soul....

SABOTAGE

I almost aborted what God birthed in me.
Repeated attempts of murder suicide.
No-longer can I hide behind the mask
No-longer can I hide the truth
I was broken and the images in my mind was distorted
All due to the false truths, painted portraits of others expectations negative motivations
Words, phrases, all the accusations contrary to the covenant of my maker
The Lord my creator.
Yet I took it all in as if their words were the first four gospels Matthew, Mark, luke and John
How did I let this happen?
Did I commit an ultimate sin worshipping idols in the form of man
I took to heart what people stated and it caused me to function in a mode of hesitation
It caused me to no longer chase my dreams and sore after my God given destiny.
The promise was compromised by someone on the inside.
Someone I held to such high esteem only to conclude they were just like me
Flesh, full of mess capable of error and sin
Looking back I saw a glimpse even then
I just ignored the signs uncertain how to address what my eyes could attest
Which has been confirmed with the plain truth
The enemy will use whomever is available for his use
The moral of the story put your trust in no man
Allow God to guide your footsteps as it is written he has the ultimate plan. (Jeremiah 29:11)

Reflect then speak...

RELIGION VERSUS RELATIONSHIP

Who would've ever thought I would find myself caught
In what I thought was a genuine relationship with my leader centered around Jesus
Yet the headship was the reason rituals and politics made the rules
Not God's law nor his ways
It was manipulation used to set the stage to disengage families and friends
Separation designed by man's hands to take full control
Who would've ever thought the same man that prayed was all along watching and lurking
Grooming me as his bait so that one day he could cross that line and make the mistake to
Attempt to have his own way with me indecently
The nerve of the enemy to think that I would even consider him sexually.
So much for a spiritual father more like a pedophilla, incest of some kind
Right down sick and distorted in his belief that I was feeble minded enough to bow down to him
Why you are merely a creep sent by the enemy.
Furthermore you had the audacity to question my position in Christ.
You fool you fake don't get it twisted all those years you was pushing religion
I was truly seeking my heavenly father's face. Living this life saved by his grace.
Sincere fasting, sincere prayers stored up for the day when the enemy thought he would use the headship to take advantage of a true saint.
It is so important to have a relationship with Christ and not just a religion filled with folks in positions
More like a dictatorship focused on controlling unconcerned about the soul winning and true deliverance.
Choose Christ not a denomination
Choose Christ not a man with his own vision and deceitful plans
Choose Christ he is that radiant light
Choose Christ he died for you and I
Choose Christ!
I did and in despite of the enemy attempt to use the headship to kill me, to try to destroy me God's agape love and his mercy covered me.
I'm so glad I have a relationship with my heavenly father through his son Jesus whose blood I declare still works!
Relationship defeats religion!

Reflect and release!

THE ANALOGY

When I was child, I spake as a child, I understood as a child, I thought as a child
But when I became a man I put away childish things
So No Longer can I go to a spiritual battle with a carnal mind and disposition
I Must take a stand and allow God to reposition me
Cause he already promised and told me
I got the victory
So more windmilling it for me
No more you hit me I'm going to hit you back,
No more upper cuts, or left hand hooks
No more holding grudges and unforgiveness, backbiting,
fussing, and fighting. I got new tactics, tools I am going to use
That the Lord has given me . To ensure I have the
victory and reach and walk in my destiny
Saints, friends, family and foes. I'm learning how to fight
Shout Lord ignite my internal light.
Which is Jesus Christ!

Reflect!

TOOL KIT

Learning how to fight.
Strategizing the attacks of the enemy.
I won't be bound because I've been set free.

    Lord,
    I thank you that on today. I am done telling folks that I will smack their faces and scratch them up!
    Lord,
    Cause i'm in tune with you and I have found in your word a clue on how to respond and what to do.
    Deuteronomy 28:7
    The Lord shall cause thine enemies that rise up against thee to be smitten before thy face, they shall come out against thee one way and flee before thee seven ways.
POW! WHAM! WHACK!
Now that's some kind of slap from the Lord that is.
So no longer am I going to sweat the small stuff nor the major attacks cause God got that!

Release!

WOUNDED SOLDIER!

Lord I know I can't run, I definitely can't hide the
scars, the wounds that keep resurfacing
They are bleeding, pus is seeping out full of infection. Hindering me from continuing in the right direction. The path I must take, God I know you don't make mistakes.
Purpose, Plan and Position.
I get it but I didn't always follow your instruction. Specifically the
one that says if you got an ought go to your brethren.
Yea, I struggled cause who the ought was with it
just didn't make sense to go tell them.
What i'm trying to say is I felt like a child trying to tell the
parent umm you hurt me. You were wrong.
I didn't really understand that you word applies to all. Even
leaders and those in positions, those that you called.
Lord,
This was such an uncomfortable position.
How does one go to the head and reprimand?
Yeah I struggle with that as a matter of fact, I buried it and let it fester
day after day. Year after year. It's been so long who's counting?

Release!

THE PLEA! THE RELEASE!

Is the infamous title of this piece....

You don't like me which is already evident and which is why you often talk about me.
So continue on with those same old sad songs, deceitful tones
Cause I'm changing the channel and staying in tuned with the Master cause I don't
have room to entertain you, it, them, they the enemy comes in various ways
But on today it is open confessions.
I stand before you today bearing witness of my pain. Some
might not like the direction in which I'm going but it's ok. I
don't write to appease you I write to free you and me.
God has snatched the very cover from this episode of hidden wounds and pains.
He has assured me that this story must be told. It is simply entitled, Let it Go!

The hurt the pain the thoughts they keep resurfacing in my brain
How you treated my child inadvertently or maybe even purposely
How you showed up to reveal your discovery of his so called hidden sin
Not one time did you offer a word of encouragement.
Instead you dwelled on his sin, had no intent to assist him recover. From issues
that he had that ran deep some steaming from his past while others you afflicted
Cause you see God's greatness in work in him just as you see it working in me.
With that being released, I must confess openly that, I forgive
you from planting weeds while God was planting seeds.
I forgive you from hating the very mention of my name reflective
of your countless attempts to scandalize my name.
I forgive you for speaking failure over the various ministries that God has birthed
in me. All because you didn't feel and see how God could use me.
I forgive you for blatantly treating me like we were
not apart of the same body of Christ!
I forgive you even now for the frowns, the expressions, the
thoughts, the conversations that will later take place that will
be full of negativity. Speaking death instead of life.
I forgive you. Those that I shared my heart, situations, complications.
Those that I let in, considered a friend, a sister, a brother and even

a mother yet you laughed and talked about me to others as you
waited patiently for me to stumble, fall short and go through.
I forgive you, especially to those that secretly hate and envy me and are
jealous of where God has me and predestined me to be. Just understand God
first choose me. Now he is molding me to be who he created me to be
I forgive you,
I forgive those of you who will later be looking at me upside my face in anger
because I have decided to escape, be set free from the bondage I've been harboring
I forgive you and I won't allow you to attach your
feelings or thoughts of me into my spirit
I just released this garbage I've been carrying
The Plea! The Release!
I just let it go!
End of story…
I'm free!

Reflect, Release and then Speak!

_____
_____
_____
_____
_____
_____
_____
_____
_____
_____
_____

THE LOVE LETTER!

Embrace the purpose for in which you were created.
Embrace your gifts and talents.
Stop running you can't hide or mask what is on the inside. It is seeping out, breaking out because it is your time. It is your season for growth, development, education, elevation, graduation.
So stop looking for folks, people to validate you when they did not create you. I did this saith the Lord! For I validated you in my Word! Phenomenal woman, Greatness, Ordination.
What more can I show you or say?
Just walk in my statutes and in my ways and the promises will manifest in you the remainder of your days.

When God speaks I listen
I'm thanking God for communing with me today in his presence I choose to stay. Covered, kept shouting Lord I accept the call, the fact you have chosen me despite my infirmities.
Speaks volume to me and displays you endless love for me.

Lord I will continue to serve thee.

Decide!

I SEE THE ENEMY!

Nothing about you is original or authentic.
You've been in competition from the beginning
You desire to be secretly the very things you despise in me when you see his glory illuminating on the scene. Christ like yeah that's my birthright
When you eyes lay upon God's purpose being done . The look that reflects is one of distress.
Your face is discombobulated While your blood is boiling you're infuriated
M.A.D. (melting in absolute devastation)
You can't phantom God's work his transformation
Yes but keep looking and you will get a confirmation.
His work ain't done but he will complete what he started in me.
I see you watching and looking.
You're waiting and lying bait hoping I fall and God's mercy is too late.
You're hoping God changes his mind and just maybe this time I won't walk in victory and I will accept defeat.
Contrary to your desires and evil intentions. God's love has and holds my attention.
So although I see you(the enemy) I just passed by you and you don't exist in the next chapter of my life's story.
I saw thc enemy!

Blindsided NOT!
Reflect and Release...

WHAT DO MEN AND WOMEN SAY THAT I AM!

Well, I been called nice/nasty. Miss know it all, I think I know more than all, even my leaders. Hmm, I've been called different ways on different days, ABC degree, CEO of America,
I've been called Bipolar And I've even been told that folks just can't deal with me. I've been called ugly, funny acting.The woman who say she saved, sanctified, holy ghost filled burning on the inside, yet her son smokes weed. The woman who barely speaks yet she say she love God. Oh she just love her four and no more.Oh her family got some mental issues. She got some things that occurred that damaged her. She ain't telling nobody but she got some issues she messed up. She tore up from the floor up! She walking around like she got it all together, anything she can do I can do it better. The conversation, "Is she an evangelist? The response. "Who her, Her, No not her."
She don't hug folks. She don't like to be touched.
Single mother of four. Don't no man want her!
She think she better than everybody else. She don't want no one riding in her car.
Ms. Business this and Ms. Business that.
As a matter of fact she make me sick.
This is what men and women really think!

The Rebuttal!

I'm so glad that man don't have the plans for my life. I found it quite interesting what man and women think yet we are supposed to be builders of the ministry. We are suppose to be helpers one to another. Instead you continue to try to kill me, murder me in hopes that the words you released concerning me will become my destiny. Jeremiah 29:11 made it very clear. So I will continue to follow his word when he says let them that have an ear hear what the spirit of the lord is saying. So when your words concerning me don't line up with God's divine plan for me I "ll just shake the very dust from my feet and keep on moving.

What men and women say don't change the purpose in which God created us in his image.

Reflect and Release!

BED OF AFFLICTION

Lord I'm bleeding out. I'm hemorrhaging.
Old wounds, scars that tore my flesh apart
Past hurt, pains things that I can't even name.
Layered in shame,blame
But I told this ole flesh that despite of the mess
I'm coming out
This revival is unique, it was designed just for me
God is snatching the very covers from what the enemy thought would smother, damage and break me. But those weights only made me stronger. It only prolonged the status and set the stage for me to take off and be in position. In despite of my opposition, plots, devices and plans. God still has his hands on me. So if I look a little funny, strange untamed. It's OK. Because when God completes the work he has begun in me. You won't recognize me.
All you will see is my Lord, my Creator, him that made me in his image.
Wait a minute, I'm in transition, So regardless of your looks, your stares, the daggers thats flying in the air.
I'm going to keep on walking and keep allowing God to peel back the layers of sin that is embedded within me. And for everyone who is wondering if I see me?
Of course I see me just as you see me but the twist is I believe what God says I will be .
I'm traveling this road called destiny.
Faith is my guide not the reflections in your eyes.
Cause it not about what you see.
As long as what I believe measures out to the size of a mustard seed. Faith!

Release!

I AM ME!

Whether you like what you see,
Whether your mind can comprehend God's destiny for me.
I am still me
Fearfully and wonderfully made
Not designed to fit into life's maze
But engineered to soar above obstacles, go beyond what man can see or think
I am created in his image
I am me
Formed in my mother's womb prior to, my father knew his purpose according to his divine plan
Even when I was a figment of my mother's imagination
He was the potter and I was in his hands merely spiritual clay in preparation to mold me shape me break me and never never forsake me.
Yeah that's God's promise.
As I stand before you today.
I don't have a melodious introduction.
I am just me.
Designed, created on this journey to fulfill my destiny.
I am me.
Unapologetically!

Speak!

MY SILHOUETTE!

My silhouette. I am so much more than that.
The outline created in his image, a unique design.
I am more than hips, thick lips, firm thighs deeper than what lies in your eyes.
You can only see a perception of me
Depending on what you perceive as reality.
Distorted image, falsified truths.
Painted on pictures of self worth.
Make up, fake butts, implants all designed to smother a brother and cause him to fall for a facade
Causing him to never come in contact with the truth
That in my nakedness, imperfections, I was designed to assist you
Help you to meet the creators expectations since the beginning of creation
Destiny awaits
But one must move beyond the flesh echoed in my silhouette.
And see me the way God intended
Again I repeat
I am so much more than that!
A Silhouette!

Reflect and release!

BREAKTHROUGH!

I forgive you
Because I'm determined to be free
I refuse to continue to hold and carry you hostage in my memories…
Flashback, rewind, deja vu, repeat, pause
I have fallen and I can't seem to get up, get out
Stuck in time.
Your face continuously flashing before my eyes
Embedded in my thoughts. So much time wasted and lost.
Feeding this unforgiveness demon.
Umm, I'm going on a strict diet.
As a matter of fact, I'm going on a fast.
No more feeding, no more eating, no more entertaining negative thoughts, time lost.
No more pampering old wounds, the hurt.
I'm letting it all go back to the pit of hell in which it belongs.
So when I see you it will be with a heart of grace, the same that God gave.
It will be in agape love.
Because learning how to love those that hurt you, will allow you to break the silence
The same silence that is often misconstrued as a killer
Will begin to kill you.
Break the silence.
Learn to love God's way.
Unconditional not according to the conditions.
Because God's love has no restrictions.

Reflect and release be set free!

I AM THAT I AM!

If God was not who He is, I would not be.
Why?
Because it's not my will but His will.
Why?
Because it's not my ways but His ways.
Why?
Because it's not about me but about His glory!
Why?
Because he created us in his image.

Reflect, release and then speak with some understanding...

LIVE!

Been hurting for some time.
Constantly replaying the episodes in my mind.
Of the countless times you deceived and betrayed our friendship.
How you spoke death through the words from your mouth with no resolve, no fault.
You meant exactly what you said.
The mistake you made was thinking that your words would leave me bleeding out, dead.
But on my bed of affliction, I made a decision to live and not die.
Instead I spoke life and cancelled every wicked contract you released in the atmosphere over my life.
I applied the tools and rebuked you!
Now I'm living this life with
joy despite what was sent to destroy God's purpose.

Because God loves me I decided to live!

Reflect then release!

INNER HEALING!

He is healing me from the inside at the very core from what occurred.
History may not change but my future is looking free from the pain that existed
Life catastrophes that had me twisted, had my mind and heart in a snare
Well I declare those obstacles are no longer there.
God removed them and only left a trace of his mercy and his grace
Each day he is rewriting my story from the lies that others told me.
Lies designed to distort the truth and smother what God really says concerning you.
As I grow I continue to recognize and see why God said let every man be a lie and God be the truth because he knew we would be criticised and ostracized and even made to believe the lies.
I'm learning that truth wears no mask while lies come baring facades.

Release!

GENERATIONAL CURSE!

This generational curse just keep showing up and plaguing the lives of the future generations.
This piece is designed to address the absence and extinction of fathers and the creation and fragmentation of families, communities and homes.

An open letter to my father JR.

When I look into my sons eyes I see the hurt he is carrying inside. I see a young boy crying out loud only no one is there to lend an ear to listen, to understand his position. No father no male example to guide him or help him. Yet I sit in the midst praying asking God to help me. Yeah cause given this situation it is an awkward position to be me. A mother who can't fix his hurts, or fix his pains. I cant even reach him in those places because it's not my vocation, nor my position to be his father or a male figure. I'm pissed and angry that you missed intricate moments in my life then and right now. When I need you the most, to be my father, my coach to help me get through these hard times to reach my son in areas that I can not comprehend all because I am not a man. I'm having mixed emotions but I must get this out and I want you to know that by no means is this written to hinder you or cause you to feel pity or self guilt. I'm releasing this burden off my heart and revealing my truth that your baby girls is hurting. Yet God is healing and setting me free from this unforgiveness.So confession is good for my soul and right now its acting as an antibiotic for this infection plaguing my soul. So I confess my faults unto you. I am angry with you! Because I've been robbed, and deprived of the privilege of having you in my life.
Then when I look into my daughter eyes it appears my past has crept into her life. WOW! No grandpa's in her life to show her what is right to pour wisdom into her life. Wisdom that she will need to assist her along her journey. JR I'm tired of improvising, picking up the pieces meeting areas that are in lack all because of someone else's slack. I know God pulled woman from Adams rib but oh my goodness I might have cracked a few bones carrying the weight of someone. LOL! God gives humor in the midst of tears. But for real all jokes aside I need you. So just know that I'M bombarding heaven with my prayers for your release. This might sound selfish but I'm sick of the enemy robbing me and my family constantly generation after generation. So I break the

cycle and snatch back my relationship with you. JR it starts with this open confusion to you. Then I move to forgiving you for how you hurt me and tore me in places that is now in need of repair full of despair. "Yet I stand Firm" this is something you would say. Just know that the God I serve is able to keep me, sustain me all in the midst of him restoring me. So I send my love unconditionally. With tears in my eyes I come out the corner, out of hiding into the light. Thanking God for his guidance.

Reflect, release then speak!

An open letter to the absent fathers and grand father's that our daughters desperately need in their upbringing.
Don't take offense just take action!

It appears my past has crept into her life.
Wow!
No grandpa's in her life to show her what is right. To pour into her life the wisdom that she will need to help her on her journey.
Father I am tired of improvising. Picking up the pieces, meeting the areas that are in lack because of someone else's slack.
I know God pulled me from Adam's rib but oh my God. I might have cracked a few bones carrying the weight of someone who was intended to compliment me.
God gives humor in the midst of the tears.
But for real, I need you!
So just know that I am bombarding heaven with my prayers for your release from prison.
Whether it's the prison of your mind or the physical incarceration from a crime committed.
Father, Papa we need thee.
I might sound selfish but i'm sick of the enemy robbing me and my family constantly. So I snatch back my relationship with you. I'm praying you into you proper position God intended you to be. The head of your family.
So this declaration starts with my true confession to you.
I was angry, hurt, broken and full of pain. Torn in places that is now in need of full repair drowning in despair. Until I realized that forgiving you set me free to love you unconditionally.
Father, Papa, Yet I stand firm in knowing the truth, that the God I serve is able to keep me, sustain me all in the midst of Him repairing me. So I send my agape love. Although with tears in my eyes I still come out of the corner, out of hiding into His marvelous light. I believe you always heard my words despite you didn't understand me and you couldn't naturally see me. But I bet you see me know in my transparency.
It's an amazing thing to connect a voice with a person with sincere understanding and empathy.
Father, Papa, it's me.
I await God's promise humbly.

Relese!

DATING IS SO OVERRATED

If you haven't claimed me.
I'm not claiming you.
See Boo or Bae
Imma take it a little bit further too.
See when you claim me, you gonna have to rename me
You got to legalize, get it right in God's eye sight
Make me your wife
See cause claim just means you declare, you profess.
Basically my brother you just talking a whole lotta mess.
I told you dating is overrated
Dating means to go out with someone whom one is romantically or sexually interested.

Reflect and speak!

I STILL GOT A PRAISE!

I got some weights on my legs, my heart is heavy and my mind is unsteady.
I'm imperfect but I still got a praise.
The enemy tried to make me think that my situation did not warrant me to praise God.
I fell short of his glory and yet he gave me daily new mercies.
I owe God total praise.
God continues to assure me that whats is damaged can be used
Yet I feel so unworthy, so undeserving of his love
I'm imperfect yet I got a praise
I'm hurting and don't know how to make it stop
I try to mask it but the hurt keep seeping out
Imperfect but yet I still got a praise

Reflect and release!

SOUL TIES

When I look back I truly thank God for my life.
How He did not let it end when I was deeply embedded in my sin.
Promiscuous, traveling various roads that all lead to dead ends.
False promises, lust in search of someone I could trust.
Misunderstood. Not realizing I could take a different course. Not realizing I had a choice.
To live and not die. To stop abusing my body self inflicted,spiritual genocide.
Wow! The things I allowed to enter my insides. Beyond my flesh and yet how wonderful it felt.
I must expose and get the true story told. That those relationships put my soul in a mode of entrapment and defeat. It gave me a yearning and a crave that set the stage and gave the enemy free range. To use me as his instrument, more like a pimp in an attempt to change my purpose. Despite those unhealthy soul ties I am yet still alive. Striving to be set free and walking in my destiny.

Reflect and Release!

THE PLOT, THE PLEA

The knot that locked that entangled
Had my mind in bondaged being strangled
No matter what I tried
I was attacked on every side, every angle feeling mangled
Unable to move yet I refused to waddle in my mess and stress about what I could of should of and obviously did not do. No time for self pity. I Knew my next move would prove that the God I serve is the truth. So i repented and asked God for his forgiveness. I surrendered and asked God to come into my life and my heart and save me. And instantly God gave me John 3:16
At that very moment God gave me life . He gave me the desire to live and not die. I realized that in despite of my past and the choices I made God's grace was sufficient and he loves me still to this day.

Release!

AN OPEN LETER TO MY PERPETRATOR.

You violated the trust. You crossed boundaries almost caused me to loose hope.
Yet the same hope I held onto commissioned me to forgive and love you.
Now I must admit that was a challenge for me.
I was commanded to love the one that hurt, attempted to tant, tamper and destroy me
I battled mentally with why he didn't deserve my mercy
Why he deserved a dismissal from access to me,to my life
My flesh demanded what he attempted in secret be told.
I wanted him to be exposed.
But God said no. Therefore my spirit looked at him as this is a soul thats in need of redemption.
I questioned myself.
Who am I not to forgive?
So I swallowed my pride.
I gave over the pain, the hurt and the shame; to the Lord
He promised t take care of me
And that He did indeed as you all can see deliverance looks good on me
So I followed the guidance of the Lord and I didn't leave .
I didn't throw in the towel
I stayed and prayed
I stayed and forgave
I stayed and loved

My perpetrator with the same love that God gives to you and me.
So now i'm walking in victory
I have closure
I have inner peace

I can smile and look him right in the face
Knowing that it was only God's grace
It was only through God's love that I was able to love because I forgave because I understand that I was forgiven

This poetic piece is for those who may have been violated; physically, mentally and emtionally broken and feel incomplete.

This is for those who was molested, raped, taken advantage of by a husband, a wife, a friend, a family member, a church leader, mentor, someone in your community, a family friend, neighbor, a teacher, a boss. Whomever, whatever title your perpetrator held, this piece is dedicated to you, those that didn't have a voice, those that felt like they didnt have a choice.

Today I give you your liberty through sharing my testimony.

Reflect and Release!

WOUNDED BY WORDS!

Experienced espionage sabotage on the verge of giving up!
Feeling as though I was hit head on with the weapontry possessing the power and force of an AK47.
It dismantled my mind left if broken into pieces.
Oh no someone else has thrown a grenade and caused a scene got me scrambling for the pieces of my sanity.
Distorted images, my self-worth clouded while everything reflects a blemish.
Who am I?
A nobody is the voice I hear in my ear as my conscious replies.
Trying to put my life back together again.
Yet the pieces don't fit, I think to myself maybe I should end my life and quit.
Nobody loves me, their words have destroyed me.
Look at me. I am all over the place.
My life is just a disgrace.
I'm at the end of my road I just can't take this anymore.
This concludes my story as others have told it.
They released this fabricated image of me into the atmosphere to ensure I wouldn't remain living.
Death awaits me.
I've been wounded by words and now I am on life support.
Gasping for air questioning Lord are you there?
Help me please. Don't let death by words be the end of my story.
I have been wounded by words yet I am still holding on.

Relect and release!

THE CAUSATION OF THE TRUTH!

The causation of the truth is all the lies that were spoken about and against you.
Released in the atmosphere to destroy your character and cause others to despise you.
Countless attempts to murder God's purpose he intends for you to produce.
Yet I find solace in the truth!
That no matter what weapons are formed, no matter what bait comes.
The lies will cause the truth to prevail and shine through.
No matter the lies. No matter the deceit and all the plots and schemes of the enemy.
It can't kill what God predestind to live in you.
It can't alter the outcome of your life story as long as you stand firm on knowing the truth!
Always remember that the truth will smother the life out of a lie.
Even those lies that come barring a disguise. God's solution will clear up the confusion.
So don't worry or fret about the pollution of lies floating in the air.
Don't worry about thoes nasty stares.
Just know that all those lies will cause the truth to honor you!

Release!

I'VE BEEN SEARCHING....

How many of you are looking for love?
How many of you want to be loved?Well I'm going to take you on this journey.
If? No. No. When you find yourself along the road cry out thank you Lord for my story being told and the enemy being exposed.
A love that never stops loving.
I've been searching.
I've been searching.
I'm on a quest.
It started when I was just a babe not old enough to leave the nest.
Straight out of my mothers womb the enemy set traps to lead me to doom.
Like when I was 2 or 3 maybe I was 5 or 6 years old.
All I can recall is that uncle, that bother, that family friend rubbing his hands up and down my legs. I just wanted to feel a warm embrace.
A hug or a kiss on my forehead or cheek but instead it was on my lips.
I knew something wasn't right especially when he showed up to tuck me in that night.
Somebody make him stop.
Somebody cut on the light.
I couldn't get him off of me, I couldn't fight!
I've been searching.
I've been searching.
Got up in my teens body developing and everything.
My mouth was so slick lips just flip. Thought I knew everything. Until momma got a new spring fling. Yeah that joker moved in so quick trying to play daddy,discipline somebody and crack the whip. I wasn't trying to hear nothing he had to say but momma always reciting her little speech," Girl you better listen to him cause providing for me." I thought to myself bills an't getting paid, disconnection notices coming every other day, but momma still getting laid. While this man cashing in and getting paid. I hated him with everything within me. Got a call one night momma said she had to work a double shift. Those were the words I thought I would never regret hearing come from momma lips. Usually that meant I could stay out late. Party with friends, do my dance and whatever else I wanted to do. I could live alittle get some experience under my belt. Because that salvation thing living for Christ requires a little bit to much dedication.

I've been searching, I've been searching for a love that never stops loving.

You know I go to church every now and again. I have religion. I believe Jesus is the son of man. I mean Jesus is God's Son. Yeah he died on the cross. He the man. He the boss. But I'm not yet ready to you know live right according to the bible. I wanted to do my own thing.

I never saw it coming. Momma ole man was trying to come up on me. He had been drinking and smoking. He grabbed my neck and started choking me and telling me that I belong to him. All I could feel was fear. I started to try to scream. While he stole my innocence as the tears rolled down my face. I knew I couldn't escape. I thought to myself. No! No! How did I let this happen to me again?

I've been searching.

I've been searching.

I thought I had a plan 18 years old man I'm free. I'm grown, I can come and go as I please and do things on my own. Now what! Yeah time for college. I'm leaving the state because I got to get as far away from momma you know? No more punishments,beatdowns,curfews, rules to break. I can stay out late. No more being momma's dudes bait. Ugh! How about I can date and not pretend the boy I like is just a friend. I can be bold and let them know yea he my man! Oh but didn't the enemy have a plan. It wasn't like I was a virgin or anything, but one wrong move and everything fell back on me. I'm talking about devastation when I should of been getting my education. What would people say about me having a baby on the way? What would people think? Not her the geek. The smart girl with the smart mouth. People had me so high up on a pedestal. I was afraid to climb down and let people see that this too was me.I was a mess. Yet I told you. I've been searching. I've been searching. When looking back I know now that all I had to do was accept God because he is love and all the things I was searching for I could have found in Him. Instead I chose to explore.

I was searching.

I was searching.

Reflect and release!

I'M BLEEDING OUT!

Oh no! Not again. How did this happen?
I must have scratched the surface.
I've punctured an old wound.
I don't think I can endure another ordel or episode.
I can't believe this is happening to me. This cant be real.
Why, oh Why?
God where are you?
I'm not strong enough to relive this anguish this stuff.
Lord not again.
The rape, the molestation, the negect, I can't bare the burdens or the traumatic effects.
Fatherless, no maternal support and the walls are closing in on me.
My mind is about to tap out!
Isolation, suffocation, devastated, the flashbacks that appear to be like deja'vue of those hands between my legs, those late nights I forcefully shared my bed. Innocence robbed. They stole my youth.
Make it stop!
I'm bleeding out!
Who can I tell this time that will listen and believe my stories?
Why? Why? Why?
Would you think that I would make this horrific account of abuse up?
The nerve of you to tell me to suck it up and go into the bathroom and wash my butt. When you don't even believe that he and she did these things to me.
Lord if you are real, I need you to wash me clean. Take everything that is causing me this pain.
I don't know how much longer I can take being submerged in this agony, this pool of pain.
I'm bleeding out!

Pause, Reflect and then release!

I'M MARRIED TO MY HUSBAND, I'M MISERABLE AND IT HURTS!

I feel deep down on the inside like someone has driven a railroad train and demolished my brain. This hurt I feel is driving me insane. I have a husband, yet I feel so alone. I'ts like I'm married to a stranger. Someone please help me I'm in danger! Can't you see me? Stop looking at the outside and see deeper. What really lies beyond this painted on smile. That's really a frown. Can't you see? The bruises and the scars? That's secretly hidden in my heart. Nolonger can I hide this truth. I need a breakthrough. My heart is heavy. Nolonger can I function and remain steady. Emotions all over the place. What can I do to make this marriage great? I've, I've tried everything I know how to do. To make my husband see me for who I am. To hold me like he knows me. Lord! I leave you with this twist. Believing you father to breath on this marriage. I insist!

Release!

I ASKED MY HUSBAND TO FORGIVE ME BUT I DIDN'T TELL HIM WHY...

Shh..
I dare not utter the details,nor the truth.
I'm just going to ask him to forgive me.
Hoping he doesn' seek the very root, of my secret sin.
That I've hidden deep within.
I vowed to never tell him but my soul can't hold it any longer.
My spirit is willing but my flesh is weak.
To tell my husband that his sweet wife has fallen short of his perception of me.
I'm so ashamed. I know I'm to blame.
Yet I'm not willing to admit to him; the very thing he always feared. It's here. It has come to pass. I feel like I'm traveling on a road entitled, "a blast from the past" Cause if I'm forced to tell the truth. Some things are gonna explode. Repeated episodes of that ole man you once were, might come back with force. Lord help me!I'm entangled in a web with a twist. Give me the mind to come forth in despite of the risk.

Release!

I DRINK AND I SMOKE TO CALM MY NERVES....

And So!
I know that smoking and drinking is not good for me
But this is my only alternative you see?
I got to do what I got to do to make it through each day.
See you don't have my troubles or you can't understand my pain.
And unless you have some realistic advise to offer you might as well keep it moving.
Cause all that hot air you releasing while you talking is nothing but pollution.
Stop talking to me like you really care.
Yeah! Yeah! I know life is not fair.
Your advice is just like welfare.
You made the mistake to give it away.
Now you want to try to dictate.
Listen!
I'm in need of someone to keep it real with me.
Cause my reality is not what you think.
I know that it has to better ways to get through these rough days.
But no one ever took the time to share with me.
How serving Christ pays.
Now let me see you unravel this mess.
While you all dignified poking out your chest.
Yeah this is a twist with a sting.
Ouch!!!
God I know you out there.
I pray you heard me.
Cause the enemy is constantly at me.
I'm twisted! Full of blisters and I'm in need of some assistance.

Release!

I'M SAVED BUT I WANT TO HAVE SEX....

I'm saved! I'm Saved!
Yet my flesh still craves, that thing called SEX.
The ole folks keep telling me baby you can be kept.
But I'm trying to tell them, all I can do is think about him.
No one in particular, cause I don't even have a mate.
So I know these thoughts are just bait.
Sent by the enemy trying to bind me up in sexual sin.
You see my soul is cryng out...
I need thee oh lord I need thee.
Someone please help me I'm trying to fight.
But it's getting really lonely lately here at night.
While I'm laying in my bed.
Trying to concentrate on the word. But instead reminiscing thoughts of days of ole
Stories never told.
Sexual pleasure, things I use to treasure and indulge in, when I was living buried in sin.
Deja'vue is taking my mind through
Vivid details, so clear. My body begins to twitch and move.
Help me to end this episode
I'm trying to hold fast to my savation
But my past has placed me in an awkward situation
Those memories need to be obsolete
I know I can't erase my past
But, Lord I need you to blot it out of my mind and I need you to do it fast!
I'm in at twist battling with things that no longer exist.

Release!

STESS AND PRESSURE

I am learning that they go hand in hand
Pounding on your brain causing distress and strain.
Making you fell like you have to make something happen or cause things to change.
Even with the problems that you face there really is no escape that you can make on your own.
Stress squeezes your brain until all your thoughts are causing pressure upon your chest and it feels like it's going to burst. You can barely catch your breath.
The anxiety buidls up into a ball of fire and then you burst into action and that causes more confusion.
Never one time did we seek help from the source.
You may be wondering who or what is the source.
The source is more powerful than any strong hold.
He can speak the word and bring forth change.
Sometimes, I been told that all we have to do is call his name and things immediately begin to happen. Situations begin to change and healing and restoration comes rapidly flowing removing all the stress and the pressure that was blocking us from believing and achieving.
Knowing that our heavenly father gave his son and his son gave his life. Jesus paid the price so we can all stand strong and endure the trials of this life. Knowing that one day we can stand before him proud to hear him say well my good and faithful servant. Through the stress and pressure of life situations and circumstances always acknowledge the relief.
He is Elohim!
He is alpha and Omega!
He is Lord of Lords!
He is Majesty!
He is the prince of Peace!
His name is Jesus!

Reflect and Release!

STRONG HOLDS!

Strongholds have some of us in a WWE choke hold.
We can't breath, we can't talk, we can't praise and we can't pray.
We haven't read or studied his word so there is nothing hidden in our heart to pull out to help us fight.
So we take the beaten.
Satan has created the illusion in our minds that he has won.
But its all an illusion cause the bible tells us that the battle is not ours its the Lords and we know that God has all power in his hands.
So who is really defeated? See satan is a cheater; he is a robber and a killer. That's the job he is equipped to do with limitations. See he places great expectations on the pursuit to kill you and I.
But God limits satan on his weapons of mass destruction. So he really does not have any control, except what we give him when we don't fast and pray and stay on our knees pleading the blood of Jesus! We are in such a hurry. We claim we are so busy and don't have time to come to church, read the bible and have a relationship in prayer with God. Yet in stead we cry and whine about the problems we often time afflict upon ourselves.
Don't allow this opportunity to pass you by to experience God on the inside working through you to release and free your soul from all those strong holds.

Reflect an Release!

PAPER

Paper you see is a very valable thing to me.
It's our means of communication you see.
I pose a question to you.
I pray you will tell the truth.
What type of father from this point on can you really be to me?
When all we have, as a means of communication is the paper you see.
Only thoughts transposed into words written from the heart on this paper is what we have.
Don't get me wrong, it means a great deal to me.
But I deserve so much more.
Will you live long enough to see the day?
When you can hold my hand, embrace me with a hug and make up for all the times I wasn't sure that you loved me.
Are you beginning to understand why this paper is so vital to me?
It's how I feel your thoughts you send.
Then I try to focus in and let them transcend into my heart and my soul.
It helps me imagine I feel your presence.
Something I can't really say I recall.
Cause you been away from me my entire life thus far.
How can I express as I address why this paper is why our relationship even exist.
Thank God for trees being in the midst.
Because If they ever become extinct
There goes our relationship like running water down the drain
Forever lost never to be reclaimed.

Reflect, breath and release!

A GOOD GUY

Oh he is a good guy.
That's what you tell yourself.
Despite it being a lie.
Don't get being good misunderstood.
Good is not acceptable by God's standard.
A man should take a stand wear the pants.
Stop walking around like he is caught in a trance.
A little bit confused, then he wants to enter into your spirit and try to convince you of what acceptable treatment looks like. Yet instead you take a beaten
When you know you desire a man that loves the Lord.
A man that can pray you through and provide for you.
In every aspect of living, spiritually, mentally and emotionally.
But what you want and what you accept is contrary in itself.
It just flat out don't make no sense you walking around all tense.
Face looking twisted, body afflicted and the truth of the matter is you addicted.
Yeah you are codependent on this good guy counterfeit pair of pants you call a man.
Stop making decisions based upon what you feel and how it looks.
Faith takes more than just reciting a scripture from the bible book.
It takes application, dedication, medication and education.
I'm talking about God's word yall!
It's sharper than a two edge sword.
Women!
Equip yourself.
That good guy notion is just another one of satan's potions he has released in the atmosphere.
To cause rubble that will make you stumble.
So you nolonger will stand and hang on to God's unchanging hand.
Remember ladies it's in Satan's plan!
A good guy is a figment of your imagination, expectation based on the flesh!
That good guy is just a joke!
As my Pastor always say, "a joke ain't nothing but a lie!"
Which is equivalent of that good guy.

Reflect and release!

VICTORY!!!

Healing is a process.
Start your journey!
I don't look like what I've been through.
Neither do you.
I don't look like what I'm going through.
It's evident that these poetic poems spoke to you.
Do yourself a favor and give yourself permission to heal.
Don't allow life circumstances, trials, and tribulations, messed up situations to stunt your growth.
Don't allow it to take you by the neck and attempt to choke the very life out of you.
Just open your mouth and speak.
As matter of fact, write your life story.
Give yourself that liberty to be free.
He did it for me
He can do it for you!
Get your breakthrough and a release!
Allow God to unravel the bondage and set you free.

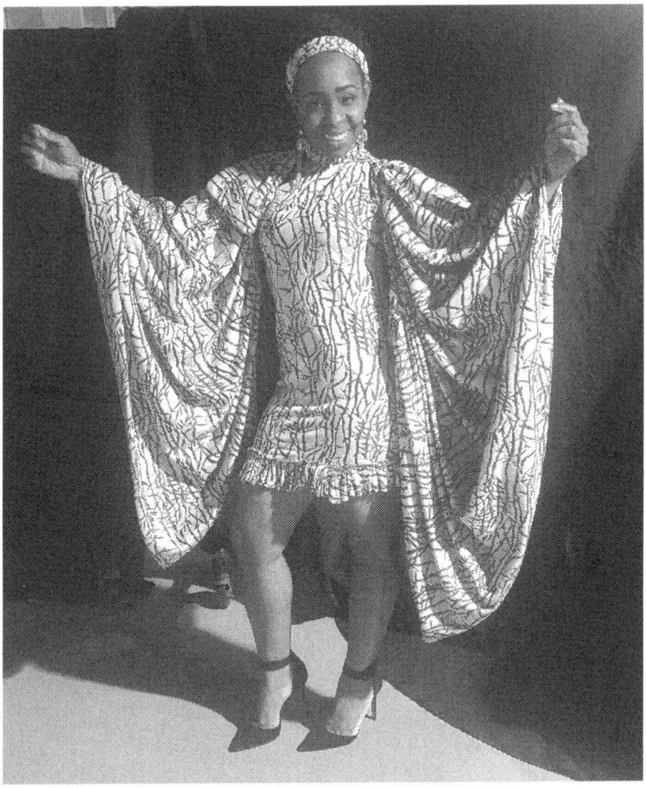

Made in the USA
Columbia, SC
01 September 2023